nickelodeon

JoJo Siwa

Style, Smile, Share!

BuzzPop

An imprint of Bonnier Publishing USA

251 Park Avenue South, New York, NY 10010

Manufactured in the United States of America LAK 0718

First Edition

1 3 5 7 9 10 8 6 4 2

ISBN 978-1-4998-0748-6

buzzpopbooks.com
bonnierpublishingusa.com

Ten Things About JoJo!

Read these ten essential facts about JoJo, then write the top ten facts about you on the following page.

3 Her birthday is May 19th.

1 JoJo has her own YouTube channel called *Its JoJo Siwa.*

2 She was born in Omaha, Nebraska.

4 She has three dogs, including her adorable Yorkie, *Bow Bow!*

5 In softball, she played catcher.

6 JoJo was named after her grandmother.

7 JoJo likes to play the piano in her spare time.

8 JoJo has one brother.

9 She began reading when she was 3 years old.

10 Her birthstone is emerald.

Ten Things About You!

BE You

1. I go to Mre

2. I have Fun

3. I hever Giv up

4.

5.

6.

7.

8.

9.

10.

SUPER CUTE

3

Bow Designer

JoJo has nearly 1,000 bows. They are everything!
Add patterns to create some cute new bows on these pages.

Try to make each one different.

Design one for your BFF!

Which one is your FAVORITE?

Super Cute

Cupcake Crazy

How cute are these cupcakes?!

Which one is different from the rest?

1

2

5

3

4

7

6

See answers on page 71.

6

Profile Style

Style your profile by filling up the following pages with info that's true to yourself and 100% all about you.

BE You

Profile Pic:
(Draw or glue in a pic.)

My Autograph:
(Write it down.)

Favorite Color:
(Color in.)

Favorite Emoji:
(Doodle it.)

Favorite Day of the Week:
(Write it down.)

Favorite Place:
(Draw or glue in a pic.)

Continued on next page.

Profile Style

BE You

Describe Your Style: *(Write it down.)*

Something Crazy:
(Doodle it.)

Something Funny:
(Draw or glue in a pic.)

Something Cute:
(Doodle it.)

Favorite Vlog:
(Write it down.)

Favorite Item of Clothing:
(Draw or glue in a pic.)

Favorite Animal:
(Draw or glue in a pic.)

Favorite Food:
(Draw or glue in a pic.)

Favorite JoJo Bow:
(Draw it on this template.)

Favorite Website:
(Write it down.)

Favorite JoJo Moment:
(Write in one sentence.)

Favorite Hashtags: *(Write them down.)*

1.

2.

3.

Favorite Thing About JoJo:
(Write in one sentence.)

Spot the Difference!

Can you find six differences between the two pictures of JoJo below?

When you find a difference, mark it on the bottom picture

FOLLOW YOUR DREAMS

SUPER CUTE

JoJo Siwa

FOLLOW YOUR DREAM

See answers on page 71.

Ice Cream Cutie!

Use your creative skills to draw the other half of this sweet ice cream, then color it in.

Give this ice cream flavor a sweet name!

BFF Code

Create a secret code to share with your BFF. Now your secrets really will be secret!

1. Write letters or symbols underneat each letter of the alphabet below.

2. Share a copy of your code with your BFF.

3. Write a message to your BFF using the code so they can decode it.

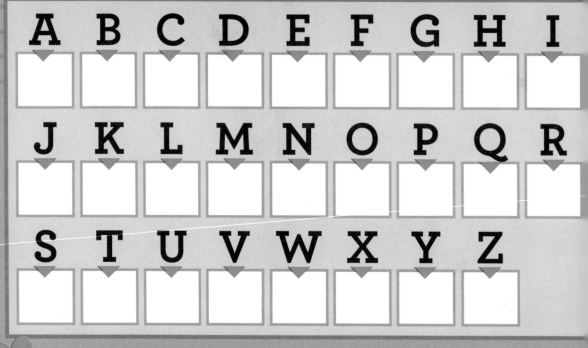

A	B	C	D	E	F	G	H	I

J	K	L	M	N	O	P	Q	R

S	T	U	V	W	X	Y	Z

Practice writing your code using JoJo's favorite phrases below. Rewrite each phrase in your code.

BOWS ARE MY SUPER POWER

SWEET IS MY SWAGGER

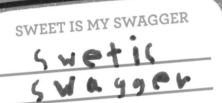

s w e t i s

s w a g g e r

DREAM CRAZY BIG

HAPPY THOUGHTS

Sweet Life

Read JoJo's awesome tips for the sweet life!

You be you!

NEVER BE AFRAID TO BE YOURSELF.

Girls never quit!

ALWAYS DO YOUR BEST, NO MATTER WHAT.

1 million starts with one

REMEMBER EVERYTHING, NO MATTER HOW BIG IT IS, HAS TO START SOMEWHE

Chill out

IT'S IMPORTANT TO TAKE SOME QUIET TIME FOR YOURSELF.

Be beautiful

BEAUTY COMES FROM THE INSIDE, SO SHINE FROM WITHIN.

Besties
not bullies

ALWAYS BE A FRIEND TO PEOPLE AND SHOW THEM KINDNESS.

Be cute and crazy

BE BOTH! BE WHATEVER YOU WANT TO BE.

What are your rules to live by? Write them down:

1. ....
....

2. ....
....

3. ....
....

4. ....
....

SWEET

15

Dance, Dance, Dance!

Can you match the poses below to the shadows on the right? Once you've matched them all, try striking a pose, just like JoJo!

1.

2.

3.

4.

5.

6.

a.

b.

c.

d.

e.

f.

g.

h.

i.

j.

TIP: THERE ARE
MORE SHADOWS
THAN THERE
ARE POSES!

Bow Bracelets

OMG! Bows really are everything. Make these sweet paper bracelets for you and your besties.

THIS IS A PERFECT ACTIVITY FOR A SLEEPOVER!

Always ask a grown-up's permission before using scissors and glue.

You will need:

★ Scissors
★ Glue   ★ Tape

Steps:

Step 1: Remove the page opposite by cutting along the dashed line.

Step 2: Cut out the bracelet strips.

Step 3: Cut out all the bows.

Step 4: Arrange the bows of your choice onto the bracelet of your choice and attach them using glue.

Tip: Place the bows a half inch apart. So cute!

Step 5: Now wrap the bracelet around your wrist and fix it in place with a piece of tape.

BOWS ARE MY SUPER POWER

Bow Hunt

JoJo can't find the bow she wants to wear. Follow the instructions to find it. Write the letter and number of the square here.

Answer:

....

Start your quest in square A-10.

MOVE:

1. **3 squares right**
2. **5 squares up**
3. **2 squares left**
4. **3 squares up**
5. **7 squares right**
6. **4 squares down**

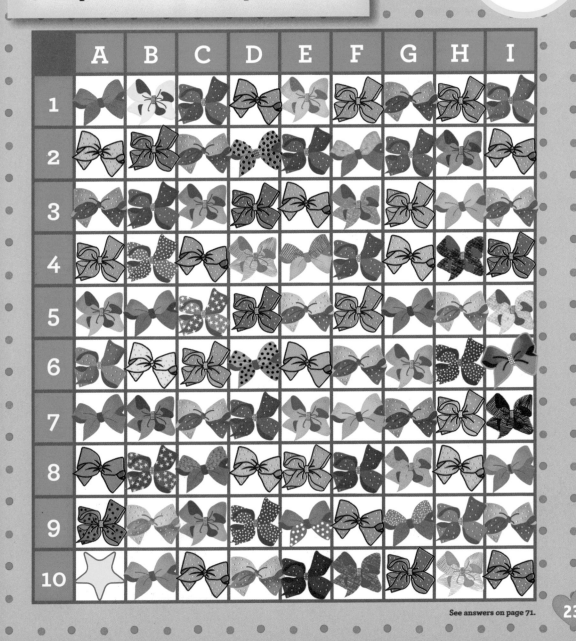

Picture Perfect

Read these simple rules for taking the best pictures, then experiment taking better shots.

1. Clean the lens on your phone or camera. Dust and dirt can make your photos misty.

2. Don't take pictures in low light – if you can't see something, then the camera won't, either.

3. Avoid bright reflections such as shiny windows, mirrors, and plastic surfaces.

4. Keep your subject big and the main focus of your picture. It's sometimes good to focus on one thing for maximum impact.

5. Keep your background free from mess for crisp, clean shots.

6. Use a flash only if necessary – natural light is way more pleasing to the eye.

7. Frame your shot. Imagine a grid on your screen to help you get everything centered. Something like this:

8. Use a backdrop when shooting objects or poses to make things really stand out.

Stick in a picture that you are very proud of showing your best pose.

Super Cute

Positive Words

JoJo's positive attitude is infectious. Can you work out what the uplifting words are below by unscrambling the letters?

BEELIVE

FENCEDCOIN

AMRED

NUF

LEGGIG

GUH

AGEMINI

KEOJ

HUGLA

KATL

See answers on page 71.

Happy Thoughts

Doodle the first thing that comes into your head in each shape after reading the prompts below. Don't hesitate; draw whatever you think of first!

Laugh

Dance

Friends

BowBow

Family

Photo Booth

29

Funny Fill-in

Have some laughs with this funny fill-in challenge. Write down the words in the list below, then fill in the blanks opposite with the words you came up with and reveal a cute and crazy letter!

1. A CELEBRITY ....
2. A PLACE ....
3. A CITY ....
4. AN ACTIVITY ....
5. AN ACTIVITY ....
6. AN ITEM TO WEAR ....
7. AN ANIMAL ....
8. TYPE OF BUILDING ....
9. A PLACE ....
10. TYPE OF FOOD ....
11. YOUR NAME ....

Choose four colors from the palette to [...] some awesome pa[...]

Flag Colo[...]

SWEET

33

Musical Match-up

Look at the big microphone picture below, then search the page opposite to find the one that matches it exactly.

BE YOUR OWN *Star*

a. b. c.
d. e. f.
g. h. i.
j. k. l.

See answers on page 71.

Smile Gallery

Give each object on this page a happy smiley face!
What makes you smile?

Things that make JoJo Smile:

BowBow	Juice
Dancing	Singing
Vlogging	Her Fans

Sweet Sequences

Sweetness overload alert!

Which sweet pic completes each sequence? Write the answer below. Tip: Pics may be used more than once.

a. b. c. d.

1

2

3

4

See answers on page 71.

Be a Stylist!

Who doesn't love dressing up?! Read the event descriptions below, then pick out the perfect outfit for JoJo on the right. How will you style JoJo?

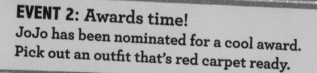

Dream huge

ANSWERS

EVENT 1: BFF time!
JoJo has been invited to a pizza and bowling party with her BFFs. Pick out the perfect outfit.

EVENT 2: Awards time!
JoJo has been nominated for a cool award. Pick out an outfit that's red carpet ready.

EVENT 3: Vlog time!
JoJo is filming a new YouTube vlog. Pick out the perfect outfit to get juiced in.

EVENT 4: Chill time!
JoJo is ready to relax. Pick out an outfit that's perfect for a laid-back Sunday at home.

What's Your Dance Style?

What type of dance best matches your personality? Find out by answering the questions below, then turn the page to reveal the answers.

ASK YOUR BESTIE TO DO THE QUIZ AND SEE HOW YOU COMPARE!

1. How would you describe your style?

a) Cool and comfy.
b) The latest trends.
c) Something that sparkles.
d) Floral and floaty.

2. Select your favorite color from the options below.

a) Blue is best!
b) Team green!
c) Gold or silver!
d) Definitely pink!

3. What do you do after school?

a) Grab some snacks.
b) Hang out with friends.
c) Watch YouTube.
d) Clubs or homework.

4. **What's most important to you in a song?**

a) The drums; you can't have a song without a beat.
b) For me, it's all about the lyrics.
c) It's 100% about the music video.
d) How a song makes you feel is EVERYTHING.

5. **What's the best thing about dancing?**

a) The music!
b) Practicing new moves and nailing them.
c) My family seeing me perform.
d) I love rehearsing until everything is perfect.

6. **Which of these could you never live without?**

a) My headphones.
b) My dance crew.
c) My dance gear.
d) My dance teacher.

Number of:	As	Bs	Cs	Ds
Me				
Bestie				

41

Quiz Answers

Mostly As

You're a break-dancer! Even though you might be relaxed when it comes to practice, you're fun, sporty, and effortlessly cool.

Mostly Bs

You're a hip-hop dancer! You're popular, fashionable, and confident, so get ready to pop and lock!

Mostly Cs

You're a tap dancer! You're fun to be around and a great person. Your friends trust you 100%.

Mostly Ds

You're a ballerina! You're graceful and a great friend! You love working hard – so ballet is perfect for you!

Dance Word Search

Find these dance-related words in the grid below!
Can you find them all?

BALLET
BREAK-DANCE
CONTEMPORARY
COUNTRY
FLAMENCO
FOLK
FOXTROT
HIP-HOP

JAZZ
JIVE
LATIN
MODERN
QUICKSTEP
TAP
WALTZ

See answers on page 71.

A	S	V	K	Y	Q	U	I	C	K	S	T	E	P	O
B	M	L	U	W	C	N	R	E	H	E	X	F	Z	K
R	O	F	A	X	T	P	O	T	L	W	B	J	C	U
F	D	L	Q	C	T	I	H	L	J	L	R	E	O	T
H	R	A	D	J	X	E	A	M	H	N	E	K	U	L
V	A	M	S	G	W	B	E	P	I	Y	A	Q	N	I
T	I	E	M	T	D	C	O	C	P	G	K	U	T	K
J	T	N	A	V	F	Y	I	S	H	X	D	Z	R	H
L	U	C	O	N	T	E	M	P	O	R	A	R	Y	D
A	Q	O	F	P	A	R	W	C	P	K	N	D	I	P
T	N	R	A	T	P	B	F	A	Z	K	C	U	K	J
I	J	G	N	P	W	C	F	V	L	K	E	G	R	I
N	Q	A	M	O	D	E	R	N	X	T	F	S	T	V
X	S	C	Z	Y	W	M	I	S	D	U	Z	J	T	E
I	H	W	P	Z	L	J	F	O	X	T	R	O	T	Z

43

Go to Bow Bow

JoJo has been away on tour and now it's time to race home to BowBow! She can't wait for a snuggle. Find the way through the maze so they can be reunited.

START

END

Be Happy

See answer on page 71.

Lyric Doodles

Play this doodle game with a friend. Take turns thinking of a song lyric, then draw it in three doodles. *Have fun guessing the lyrics!*

1

I can't
Kum
back
likr a boomay

2

3

Guess the lyrics here:

....

....

Now, reveal the lyrics here:

....

....

46

1

2

3

Guess the lyrics here:

....

....

Now, reveal the lyrics here:

....

....

1

2

3

Guess the lyrics here:

....

....

Now, reveal the lyrics here:

....

....

Cute Patchwork

Doodle cute things into each square of this grid to create a cute patchwork masterpiece.

Bow Bow should totally make the grid!

48

Happy Playlist

JoJo knows that music is an awesome way to get you feeling great. It can literally lift your mood. What songs would make your happy playlist?

A SONG THAT MAKES YOU SMILE:

....

....

A SONG THAT MAKES YOU
WANT TO DANCE:

....

....

A SONG THAT REMINDS YOU
OF A SUPER-HAPPY TIME:

....

....

A SONG THAT YOU LOVE TO SING:

....

....

A SONG THAT YOU AND YOUR
BEST FRIEND BOTH LOVE:

....

....

Doodles

Draw the first thing that comes into your head when you read these hashtags.

#Fun

#JoJoSiwa

#Summer

#Love

#Peaceouthaterz

SUPER CUTE

50

Positivity Cards

Don't you just love JoJo's positive vibes and attitude? If you or a friend aren't feeling 100%, then cut out these positivity cards and read or share one together when you're feeling down.

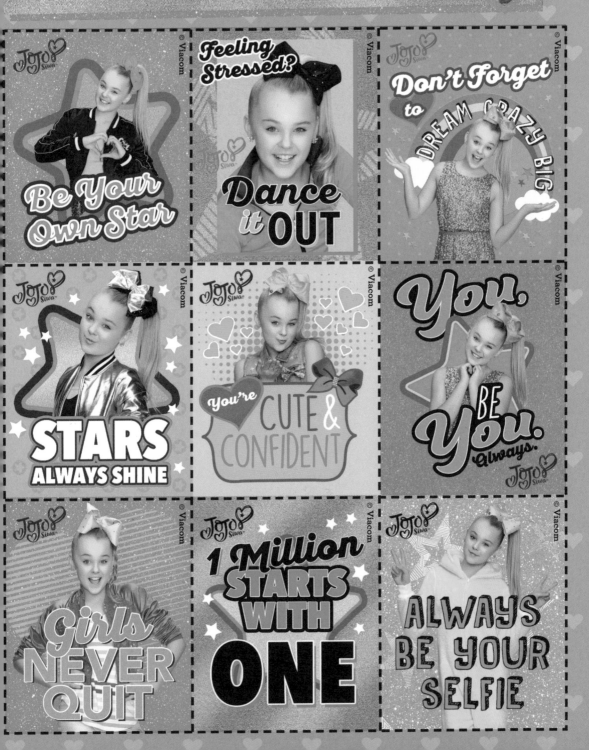

Positivity Cards

If you're feeling down, it's always helpful to tell someone, whether it's a friend, parent, or even a teacher. A problem shared is a problem halved. It's good to talk!

DREAM
Crazy
BIG

JoJo dreamed of becoming a star when she was just a little girl and worked hard to turn her dream into reality. Use the space below to write about your dreams for the future.

My Dream:

JOB

....

....

VACATION

....

....

OUTFIT

....

....

DAY

....

....

MEAL

....

....

Express Yourself!

Some weeks can be **SO** busy that life feels crazy sometimes. How was your week? Color in each unicorn to represent your moods this week. There's one for every day!

BE YOU

Monday: ....
....
....
....

Tuesday: ....
....
....
....

Wednesday: ....
....
....
....

56

Thursday: ....
....
....
....

Hanging out with friends is a super way to relax and be yourself.

Friday: ....
....
....
....

Saturday: ....
....
....
....

Which day did you feel the best and why?

Sunday: ....
....
....
....

57

Ice Cream Creator!

Use the color code to create the ultimate ice cream cones for friends and family.

Create your own flavors on the blank scoops.

Create one for JoJo, too!

Code:

Chocolate

Strawberry

Cotton Candy

Vanilla

Mint Chocolate Chip

Add some toppings!

59

Discover Your Juice!

As you know, JoJo loves juice, especially when it's poured over her head. What type of juice are you and your friends? Read the descriptions, then match names to the juices.

JUICE TYPE: Fizzy
DESCRIPTION: This person is always bubbling with happiness.
THIS JUICE BELONGS TO:

....

JUICE TYPE: Fruity
DESCRIPTION: This person has a zest for adventure.
THIS JUICE BELONGS TO:

....

JUICE TYPE: Sweet
DESCRIPTION: This person is filled with kindness.
THIS JUICE BELONGS TO:

....

JUICE TYPE: Iced
DESCRIPTION: This person is the coolest and a trendsetter.
THIS JUICE BELONGS TO:

....

JUICE TYPE: All the flavors
DESCRIPTION: This person is totally crazy, out there, and fun!
THIS JUICE BELONGS TO:

....

Writing Challenge!

Choose happy words from the selection below and then write your own song or poem. Share it with a friend or keep it for yourself.

Sunshine	Unicorn
Stars	Weekends
Smile	Books
Cake	Adventures
Peace	Friends
Laugh	Butterfly
Joy	Fluffy
Rainbow	Sweet
Puppy	Kindness
	Love

A Bow For Every Day

Create a bow with a different pattern or doodle for each day of the week. Think about your favorite JoJo styles as you draw.

Monday

Tuesday

Wednesday

Thursday

Friday

Saturday

Sunday

Super Snippets

Can you describe your favorite memories in one sentence? Make every word count!

Vacation

....

....

....

Party

....

....

....

Birthday

....

....

....

Holiday

....

....

....

School

....

....

Follow the instructions and doodle what you see in the boxes.

Look up!

Something you can touch.

Look down!

Something that
reminds you
of JoJo.

Something
hidden.

Try this activity
in a place you find
inspiring!

Spin around
and stop.

Doodle Diary

Doodle something onto each day of the month to express how you felt. Use the code, or create your own.

HAPPY =   EXCITED =

SAD =   RELAXED =

STRESSED =   CRAZY =

1

2

3

4

5

6

7

8

9

10

11

12

13

14

15

16

17

18

19

20

21

22

23

24

25

26

27

28

29

30

31

Be Your Own Star

Fill each star with a different pattern or doodle. Think about your hopes and dreams as you draw.

Create Positive Banners!

Write your own inspiring words onto the flags and banners, just like the one below JoJo.

Girls **NEVER QUIT**

Super

Bestie Temporary Tattoos!

Don't you just love your JoJo temporary tattoos? If you were to give these temporary tattoos to your besties, who would get what? Write their names next to the temporary tattoos that best suit them.

You can give more than one temporary tattoo to a bestie!

BE You

BE You

Super Cute

DREAM Crazy BIG

Dream huge

EAT. DANCE. SLEEP. JoJo Siwa

JoJo Siwa

SWEET IS MY SWAGGER

From My Heart

SUPER CUTE

SWEET

DREAM CRAZY BIG

SWEET

CUTE & CONFIDENT

Temporary tattoos and instructions are at the back of the book.

Answers

Page 6: Cupcake Crazy
Cupcake 3 is different from the rest.

Page 10: Spot the Difference!

Pages 16-17: Dance, Dance, Dance!
1. a 2. h 3. j 4. i 5. e 6. c

Page 23: Bow Hunt
The answer is square I-6.

Page 26: Positive Words
BEELIVE > BELIEVE
FENCEDCOIN > CONFIDENCE
AMRED > DREAM
NUF > FUN
LEGGIG > GIGGLE
GUH > HUG
AGEMINI > IMAGINE
KEOJ > JOKE
HUGLA > LAUGH
KATL > TALK

Pages 34-35: Musical Match-up
The matching picture is f.

Page 37: Sweet Sequences

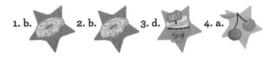

1. b.   2. b.   3. d.   4. a.

Page 43: Dance Word Search

A	S	V	K	Y	Q	U	I	C	K	S	T	E	P	O
B	M	L	U	W	C	N	R	E	H	E	X	F	Z	K
R	O	F	A	X	T	P	O	T	L	W	B	J	C	U
F	D	L	Q	C	T	I	H	L	J	L	R	E	O	T
H	R	A	D	J	X	E	A	M	H	N	E	K	U	L
V	A	M	S	G	W	B	E	P	I	Y	A	Q	N	I
T	I	E	M	T	D	C	O	C	P	G	K	U	T	K
J	T	N	A	V	F	Y	I	S	H	X	D	Z	R	H
L	U	C	O	N	T	E	M	P	O	R	A	R	Y	D
A	Q	O	F	P	A	R	W	C	P	K	N	D	I	P
T	N	R	A	T	P	B	F	A	Z	K	C	U	K	J
I	J	G	N	P	W	C	F	V	L	K	E	G	R	I
N	Q	A	M	O	D	E	R	N	X	T	F	S	T	V
X	S	C	Z	Y	W	M	I	S	D	U	Z	J	T	E
I	H	W	P	Z	L	J	F	O	X	T	R	O	T	Z

Pages 44-45: Go to BowBow